[H.A.S.C. No. 114–88]

RECOMMENDATIONS FROM THE NATIONAL COMMISSION ON THE FUTURE OF THE ARMY

HEARING

BEFORE THE

SUBCOMMITTEE ON TACTICAL
AIR AND LAND FORCES

OF THE

COMMITTEE ON ARMED SERVICES
HOUSE OF REPRESENTATIVES

ONE HUNDRED FOURTEENTH CONGRESS

SECOND SESSION

HEARING HELD
FEBRUARY 10, 2016

U.S. GOVERNMENT PUBLISHING OFFICE

98–916   WASHINGTON : 2016

SUBCOMMITTEE ON TACTICAL AIR AND LAND FORCES

MICHAEL R. TURNER, Ohio, *Chairman*

FRANK A. LoBIONDO, New Jersey
JOHN FLEMING, Louisiana
CHRISTOPHER P. GIBSON, New York
PAUL COOK, California
BRAD R. WENSTRUP, Ohio
JACKIE WALORSKI, Indiana
SAM GRAVES, Missouri
MARTHA McSALLY, Arizona
STEPHEN KNIGHT, California
THOMAS MacARTHUR, New Jersey
WALTER B. JONES, North Carolina
JOE WILSON, South Carolina

LORETTA SANCHEZ, California
NIKI TSONGAS, Massachusetts
HENRY C. "HANK" JOHNSON, Jr., Georgia
TAMMY DUCKWORTH, Illinois
MARC A. VEASEY, Texas
TIMOTHY J. WALZ, Minnesota
DONALD NORCROSS, New Jersey
RUBEN GALLEGO, Arizona
MARK TAKAI, Hawaii
GWEN GRAHAM, Florida
SETH MOULTON, Massachusetts

JESSE TOLLESON, *Professional Staff Member*
DOUG BUSH, *Professional Staff Member*
NEVE SCHADLER, *Clerk*

CONTENTS

Page

STATEMENTS PRESENTED BY MEMBERS OF CONGRESS

WITNESSES

APPENDIX

RECOMMENDATIONS FROM THE NATIONAL COMMISSION ON THE FUTURE OF THE ARMY

———

House of Representatives,
Committee on Armed Services,
Subcommittee on Tactical Air and Land Forces,
Washington, DC, Wednesday, February 10, 2016.

The subcommittee met, pursuant to call, at 2:00 p.m., in room 2118, Rayburn House Office Building, Hon. Michael R. Turner (chairman of the subcommittee) presiding.

OPENING STATEMENT OF HON. MICHAEL R. TURNER, A REPRESENTATIVE FROM OHIO, CHAIRMAN, SUBCOMMITTEE ON TACTICAL AIR AND LAND FORCES

Mr. TURNER. The hearing will come to order. We have votes that are coming up, so we are going to try to get through our opening statements, General Ham's opening statement, and then return for questions.

So the subcommittee meets today, along with members of the full committee, to receive testimony on the findings and recommendations of the National Commission on the Future of the Army [NCFA]. I would like to welcome our distinguished panel, General Carter Ham, U.S. Army, retired, Chairman of the Commission appointed by Chairman Thornberry, and the Honorable Robert F. Hale, the commissioner appointed by Ranking Member Smith. Mr. Hale was also the lead for the Commission's subcommittee on aviation issues.

The Congress was prompted to form the Commission in large part over two major concerns. The first was how the Army should best organize and employ the total force in a time of declining resources. The second was whether the Army should proceed with the transfer of AH–64 Apache aircraft from the Reserve Components to the Regular Army, as directed by the Army's Aviation Restructure Initiative, ARI.

The Commission reported its findings to Congress and the administration on January 28, 2016, and made 63 recommendations, 19 of which were directed towards Congress for potential action. This will provide the committee with enough time to review the recommendations as the committee prepares to mark the National Defense Authorization Act for 2017.

In considering recommendations, the Commission was instructed to take into account, quote: "anticipated mission requirements for the Army at acceptable levels of national risk in a manner consistent with available resources and anticipated future resources."

I want to underscore those last two, because it is a significant limit upon the Commission's view, and that was available resources and anticipated future resources.

Consequently, the Commission assumed that the Army budget is flat-lined at the fiscal year 2016 Presidential budget levels. The Commission has indicated that a total force Army of 980,000 soldiers is an acceptable level of risk, but is the lowest total end strength the Army can go given mission requirements and the current defense strategic planning guidance. Again, the Commission did not consider the potential for budget increases over the amount of the fiscal year 2016 Presidential budget.

However, the Commission did acknowledge that the current defense guidance does not include emerging threats such as Russian aggression and the growing threat of ISIL [Islamic State of Iraq and the Levant]. The Commission then further notes that perhaps, quote, their "greatest concern is the inadequacy of that guidance."

We have heard senior military leaders testify before this committee that our military is operating at the "ragged edge" and that current assumptions in the defense guidance are rosy at best. Here is what we know. The Army is being asked to do more with less. Demands from the combat commands for Army capabilities and capacity continue to increase. The world's security environment is considerably worse now than when the Department of Defense conducted its more recent Quadrennial Defense Review in 2014.

Going beyond just Russia and ISIL, North Korea conducted another ballistic missile test over the weekend. The Army has soldiers deployed in over 140 countries. The Army has provided over 1.5 million troop-years to the wars in Iraq and Afghanistan since 2001. And the Army has nearly 100,000 soldiers committed to the Pacific and continues to deter aggression in the Korean peninsula. However, despite these demands, the Army has continued to downsize and budgets have been reduced.

I hope today we can engage in candid discussion regarding total Army force capability and capacity as compared to the current and emerging threats. I want to briefly touch on the Army's Aviation Restructure Initiative, or ARI.

Originally, the ARI had proposed numerous changes to Army aviation capacity, including the transfer of all Apache helicopters out of the Army National Guard to the Regular Army. The Commission examined three comprehensive options for the Army's ARI, and we look forward to hearing more details about their final recommendations. This should also provide a great opportunity for the committee to gain a better understanding of the Commission's views in how to better utilize the Reserve Components.

Before we begin, I would like to return to my good friend and colleague, Niki Tsongas, for her opening remarks.

[The prepared statement of Mr. Turner can be found in the Appendix on page 33.]

STATEMENT OF HON. NIKI TSONGAS, A REPRESENTATIVE FROM MASSACHUSETTS, SUBCOMMITTEE ON TACTICAL AIR AND LAND FORCES

Ms. TSONGAS. Thank you, Mr. Chairman, and good afternoon to our witnesses. I appreciate you both being here.

The National Commission on the Future of the Army had an ambitious task, and I commend the commissioners—the two of you—and their staff for the work they put into this report. I would also like to thank the chairman for opening the hearing to the full committee, as these topics impact the men and women of our Army stationed across the country and around the world.

As many of us in this hearing have heard before, the Army is being asked to do more with less against an array of diverse and complex global threats. These constraints require the Army, the Department of Defense [DOD], and Congress to closely examine the appropriate distribution of active Guard and Reserve forces, as well as the right mix of capabilities needed to defend the United States and its allies.

Today's challenges also require the Army to ensure that it is optimizing the performance of its soldiers to see that they remain the best trained and best equipped force in the world.

The Commission's recommendations appear to fall into three broad categories. First, the Commission made specific recommendations regarding the size, location, and composition of the Army. Second, the Commission report makes many recommendations on how to further integrate the Reserve Components of the Army, the National Guard and Army Reserve, with the Regular Army. Finally, the report includes recommendations on the future of Army aviation, and in particular the question of where Apache helicopters should reside.

I look forward to hearing more details about how the Commission reached its conclusions on all these topics. I would also like to hear more about the cost associated with the Commission's recommendations. If Congress chooses to pursue any of the recommendations in the report, the money will have to come from somewhere, either within the Army or from another military service's budget.

Fully understanding these potential tradeoffs is a critical part of considering the Commission's recommendations. These are not easy decisions to make, and I appreciate the opportunity to have a robust debate here in Congress on the way forward. I look forward to hearing more about how you arrived at some of your key recommendations.

Thank you. And with that, I yield back.

Mr. TURNER. Thank you, Congresswoman Tsongas.

I ask unanimous consent that non-subcommittee members be allowed to participate in today's hearing after all subcommittee members have had an opportunity to ask questions. Is there objection? Without objection, non-subcommittee members will be recognized at the appropriate time for 5 minutes.

With that, General Ham.

STATEMENT OF GEN CARTER HAM, USA (RET.), CHAIRMAN, NATIONAL COMMISSION ON THE FUTURE OF THE ARMY, AND HON. ROBERT F. HALE, COMMISSIONER, NATIONAL COMMISSION ON THE FUTURE OF THE ARMY

General HAM. Thank you, Mr. Chairman, and Ms. Tsongas, thank you very much. On behalf of all my fellow commissioners and the great staff that support us, I thank you for inviting me and

Secretary Hale to testify before the committee on a report on the future of the Army.

The committee and your staff have already received the Commission's report, so I won't spend a lot of time addressing specific points. But I would like to give you a sense of how we approach the task that you gave to us in the fiscal year 2015 National Defense Authorization Act [NDAA].

The Commission made every effort to be inclusive, accessible, and transparent. We visited 17 States and interacted with over 320 different Army units across all 3 components. We interacted with all 54 adjutants general and with 33 Governors. About 80 Members of Congress engaged with the Commission, as well, and we met with all 6 geographic combatant commanders and many of our most important allies and foreign partners, and that frankly is only a partial list of our engagements.

As Chairman Turner indicated, we paid strict attention to the law you passed creating the Commission. Importantly, our recommendations had to be consistent with, I quote: ''acceptable levels of national risk and anticipated future resources.''

In other words, we simply were not unbounded in our work.

The result is a set of 63 specific recommendations that we believe are well researched, based on realistic assumptions, and backed by solid data. First, America's Army is the best in the world. Those who wear the uniform deserve our gratitude each and every day. But even those great men and women serving in uniform, the Army faces severe challenges, many of them budget-driven.

From fiscal years 2010 to 2015, overall defense spending declined 7 percent, but Army funding declined 14 percent. On the two main issues before the Commission—force size and mix and the Apache transfer—the Commission found the following. An Army of 980,000 is the minimally sufficient force to meet current and anticipated missions at an acceptable level of national risk. Within that 980,000, the Commission finds the Regular Army should be 450,000, an Army National Guard of 335,000, and the Army Reserve at 195,000, represent the right mix of forces and, again, the absolute minimum levels to meet America's national security objectives.

To fully understand this recommendation, it is important to remember again the mandate that you gave us. We were tasked to size the force in light of the two previously mentioned considerations—acceptable risk and anticipated resourcing. Adjust either or both of those and you would reasonably arrive at very different conclusions. In our assessment, an Army of 980,000 is again the absolute minimum; a floor, not a ceiling.

On the Apache question, the Commission recommends the Army maintain 24 manned Apache battalions, 20 in the Regular Army and 4 in the Army National Guard. The Commission recommendation has advantages over the Aviation Restructure Initiative in both wartime capacity and surge capacity and it will reduce peacetime deployment stress. It will also, in our view, promote better integration of the Regular Army and the Army National Guard.

To offset the cost of having four Apache battalions in the Guard, the Commission suggests that the Army add only two Black Hawk battalions to the Guard instead of the four that are currently planned, and we recommend some slowing of Black Hawk modernization.

The report also contains several prominent themes based on the Commission's fact-finding and analysis. The Commission considers sustaining the All-Volunteer Force vital to the future of the Nation. A return to a draft or other model of compulsory military service will not yield the quality Army the Nation requires, but an All-Volunteer Force is expensive to recruit and retain. We believe doing so is the right choice.

The Commission believes it is critically important to develop a true total force culture. While the Regular Army, the Army National Guard, and the Army Reserve are distinct, essential, and interdependent, they are meant to operate as one force, with their efforts fully integrated. We found gaps and seams that exist in the implementation of the total force policy, and our report highlights some of those and offers some remedies.

For example, we recommend putting all Army marketing under one office, fielding a consolidated pay and personnel system, and making changes to the existing section 12304b authority that will make it easier for the Army to employ the Reserve Components. The Commission recommends funding at the President's fiscal year 2016 level, which would provide the Army with the minimum resources necessary to meet its requirements and acceptable levels of risk.

But given the evolving strategic environment and the potential for growing instability, even this level of funding may prove inadequate. Additionally, Army funding must be predictable. Successive years of budget uncertainty and continuing resolutions have had significant negative consequences for the Army.

It should be understood that in the Commission's view even with budgets at the President's budget for fiscal year 2016, the Army would still suffer from some significant shortfalls in aviation and short-range air defense, as well as other capabilities that we address in the report.

That is a very brief rundown of what we found. Certainly not everyone will agree with our recommendations. Indeed, many have already voiced their disagreement. What I do hope, though, is that our report will contribute to the important debate that you and the Congress and the administration and the Army—indeed, the Nation—must have to determine how America's Army should be sized, trained, modernized, and postured.

With that, Secretary Hale and I are prepared to answer your questions.

Thank you.

[The prepared statement of General Ham can be found in the Appendix on page 36.]

Mr. TURNER. Thank you, General. It is our honor to have our chairman with us today, and I recognize Chairman Thornberry.

The CHAIRMAN. Thank you, Mr. Chairman. I just want to take a moment—and I know I speak on behalf of Mr. Smith, as well—to express our appreciation to General Ham and to Mr. Hale for their willingness to serve on this Commission, as well as the work that the Commission has done, as well as the staff that have made all this possible.

I think that you all have done exactly what we asked you to do in answering some very specific questions, but as General Ham was just referring, you have also set up some of the larger discussion that we need to pursue, such as how we make sure all the components of the Army work together in a total force.

So I think this is very good and very important work, and I just want to express appreciation to the work of the commissioners and the staff. In a relatively short amount of time, you have dealt with some very big issues. So thank you.

And I would yield back.

Mr. TURNER. Thank you, Mr. Chairman. I, too, want to thank both of you for the work that you have done. And it is incredibly helpful to us. We also need to look at it in the context of the limitations that you were given in putting the construct together.

And so with that, General Ham, I have a question for you. It wasn't within your charge. You were constrained and limited by budget caps. But I would ask if you could opine, if Congress did have additional funds to allocate, would you recommend that Congress stop the Army drawdown? General Ham.

General HAM. Yes, thanks, Mr. Chairman. As the Commission did not look at that issue specifically, let me speak personally rather than as chairman of the Commission. It is my view that with additional funding, were additional funding to be available, some of the capability shortfalls that we mentioned in the report, some in aviation, short-range air defense, missile defense, military police, wheeled vehicle transport, and some other capabilities would be highly beneficial to the Army and would reduce the risk that we assessed given the size of the force that we recommended.

So I think that is where additional capability, additional capacity would buy down risk over time. And maybe Secretary Hale has some thoughts.

Mr. HALE. May I briefly on the budget side of this? The budget that was released yesterday has less resources—and I think you all know—for the Army and DOD than was in the fiscal year 2016 budget plan, by a significant amount. So we are already off the track that the Commission assumed in terms of funding for DOD. And I think the Commission feels strongly we need to get back on that track in 2018 and beyond, and 2017 if that is possible.

Mr. TURNER. Thank you. General Ham, of course, I am referring to the total force drawdown numbers. In your report, you have said what the force needs to do, and you have said what some of the threats are as to how that force can be utilized. But as you know, the total force drawdown is based on budgetary constraints that you were given.

If Congress had the resources and we could stop the drawdown of the total force numbers, should we?

General HAM. Mr. Chairman, I believe doing so would be wise, and it would afford the Army the opportunity to gain some of those capabilities that are currently in shortfall. The one caveat that I would offer, Mr. Chairman, is it is not just about the size. The size is important. But the size of that force, that Army must be properly modernized, trained, and resourced. So it is not just the number. It is all——

Mr. TURNER. But, General, let me interrupt you for just a second. I understand that what you are saying is that in addition to having the force numbers, you have to have resources, you have to have training, you have to have capability for those force numbers. But I appreciate your statement that the total force number does matter and that if we had the resources, your recommendation it'd be that we not draw the force down, but that we also in addition to it adequately equip it, train it, and provide it with capability.

General HAM. That is correct, Mr. Chairman. I agree with that.

Mr. TURNER. Okay, thank you. One other question, and then I will turn to Congresswoman Tsongas.

In looking to Europe, Lieutenant General Ben Hodges, Commanding General of Army Europe, has stated that there used to be 300,000 soldiers in Europe during the height of the Cold War. Today we have 30,000 distributed all over Central and Eastern Europe with the same mission—to assure allies and to deter Russia, just like we did in the Cold War, according to General Hodges.

There is a big difference in capability and capacity between 300,000 and 30,000. General Ham, could you elaborate on the Commission's reasoning for recommending number 14, to realign an ABCT [armored brigade combat team] back to Europe? And could you give the committee your thoughts on whether this should be a permanent station or rotational unit?

General HAM. Thanks, Mr. Chairman. Our recommendation is that an armored brigade combat team be forward stationed, assigned to Europe, rather than the current model of rotational forces. Rotational forces are certainly capable and offer a lot to the command, but it is our assessment that stationing an armored brigade combat team in Europe has two effects.

One, it conveys a sense of permanence and commitment, which is helpful both in deterrence and in assurance. But secondly, we found in the larger sense that the Army's nine—the Regular Army's nine armored brigade combat teams are totally consumed in the current rotational model, which has rotational armored brigades to Korea, that basically is three to make one, to the Mideast, three to make one, and Europe, three to make one, which means all nine armored brigade combat teams in the Regular Army are committed, leaving no capacity for an unforeseen contingency.

If the Army were allowed to forward station an armored brigade combat team in Europe, that would provide not only positive effects on deterrence and assurance, but it would provide some residual capacity to the Army for an unforeseen contingency.

Mr. TURNER. Thank you. We are going to pause. Votes have been called. I thank both of you for your patience. But we will be returning for additional questions after the votes. That will be recess.

[Recess.]

Mr. TURNER. Thank you. We will resume the hearing and turn to Congresswoman Tsongas.

Ms. TSONGAS. Thank you, Mr. Chairman. I wanted to follow up. You have issued 63 total recommendations, and close to 20 of those were directed towards Congress that we needed to act. But I am curious how you would rank order them, if there are some that you see more pressing and others that could be addressed later. And I will start with you, General Ham.

General HAM. Thanks, ma'am. We purposely did not prioritize the recommendations, but I think—I will offer my thoughts on ones that perhaps might require a little more attention than others. For me, it would begin with the very first recommendation that says maintain and sustain the All-Volunteer Force, and clearly, Congress's role in that is absolutely essential. I think, frankly, if we don't do that, the rest of it almost doesn't matter, because we have got to have the quality women and men to join the Army that are necessary.

Secondly, I would emphasize the Congress's role in assuring prediction and responsible budgeting for the Army. I think that is absolutely vital to give that element of stability and predictability to the Army in its funding processes.

Thirdly, there are a number of recommendations that address specific actions that cause the total force policy to be implemented more fully. Some of those require some legislative change, and so I would group those total force recommendations perhaps as a next priority for the Congress to address.

And again, just the larger recommendation with regard to the size and readiness of the force, the 980,000 at required levels of readiness, I think that would obviously also rank very, very high.

Ms. TSONGAS. Secretary Hale, would you agree with that? Or would you have a slightly different prioritize?

Mr. HALE. No, I agree with it. I want to underscore the need for predictable budgets. This turmoil is just eating the time of senior leaders and the Congress, I might add.

Let me just give a couple of examples of the last theme that General Ham raised, and that is integrating into the total force. I think the Apache recommendation actually fits within this category. And that if you follow the Commission's recommendation, there will be one other area of connective tissue between the Guard and the Regular Army.

But the recommendations on multicomponent units are also I think very important. The Army is already doing this, but I think the Commission believes they could do more. And we made some specific suggestions for a pilot program in aviation that could lead to more multicomponent units. And there are a number of others, like integrated recruiting.

So there are several, I think, specific ideas that fit within the theme that General Ham raised of integrating the Regular Army and the Guard in a better manner.

Ms. TSONGAS. Did you identify costs associated with that integration? And how did you—or not? And if so, how would you pay for them? Were there tradeoffs you would make in favor of that, moving forward in that way?

General HAM. Ma'am, the one area where we tried to address costs specifically as to tradeoffs was in the aviation realm. For the other recommendations, we did not. Frankly, time and capacity of the staff and expertise, we did not have the time to offer specific cost findings with many of the other recommendations. I am seated next to the cost expert, as you know.

Mr. HALE. A title I am trying to shed.

Ms. TSONGAS. Mr. Secretary, you might have some off-the-top-of-your-head idea of cost.

Mr. HALE. No, I think I won't go there. But I will say, in the aviation area, we did do costing there, that Congress specifically tasked us to look at the Apache transfer. And the—although the Commission's recommendation adds to capacity and peacetime capabilities, it does add to costs, about $165 million a year in operating costs and around $400 million in one-time procurement costs.

And we did offer what we called an illustration of ways to offset that cost through a slight decrease in the size of the Black Hawk fleet and a modest slowdown in a modernization of the fleet. It is not that Black Hawks aren't important; they are. But they are a large fleet, and we felt that it was more important, if you had to offset the costs, it was more important to accomplish the Apache transfer even if some offsets had to be made.

And there were some other general offsets that were discussed, as well. So we certainly paid attention to costs. Although as General Ham said, outside of aviation, we did not specifically cost each option.

Ms. TSONGAS. At least it is an acknowledgement that there are costs associated with this and that in the world of constrained resources that as we move forward we are going to have to think about that as we implement or not some of these recommendations——

Mr. HALE. But some of them won't add to cost. I mean, for example, the multicomponent units, if you use the same units—I mean, unless you add the units—you won't significantly add to costs. I think some of the things can be done without significantly added costs, and I would hope that when you see the Army's response that they will identify some of those for you.

Ms. TSONGAS. I have a follow-on question. In the end, in an All-Volunteer Force, in any Army, it comes down to the people that you are able to attract. And what I would like to do—one of the recommmendations was you want to stop cuts in the overall size of the Army. But even if this was followed, our troop levels will still be at the lowest levels in decades. So that is why I do think that those you do have are of the highest caliber.

So how can the Army continue to improve the physical, the psychological, the cognitive, the overall human performance of the force to make sure that those that you are attracting are able to perform at the highest level and you make the most of every soldier?

General HAM. Thanks, ma'am. As you know, that was not a specific charge to the Commission to look at that issue. So if you will allow me to step away from my role as chairman and speak perhaps to some of the things that we observe throughout the force.

The young women and men of the Army, all three components, Regular Army, Army National Guard, Army Reserve, what we heard loud and clear is that they joined to serve. They want to be utilized. So that is part of, I think, the recruiting and retention challenge for a quality force is use that force.

We heard—this is anecdotal—but we heard from a number of young soldiers, mid-grade soldiers, particularly in the Reserve Components, that if they weren't going to be utilized, if they weren't going to be operationally employed, well they might choose to do something else. So I think that has an important part of it.

I think a second component to successful recruiting and retention is that the young people who we've had the great fortune to engage with across the Army, they want to feel like what they are doing makes a difference, that they are making a valuable contribution. Certainly they are concerned about compensation; that is certainly an important piece of this. But it is not only the piece. It is not the only piece of their sense of service.

And so I think it is this combination of challenge, of importance of mission, combined with the proper level of compensation that will allow the Army to continue to attract in an admittedly declining pool of eligible women and men across the country to serve, but will continue to attract the bright young people that the Nation needs in its Army to maintain its vitality and effectiveness.

Ms. TSONGAS. Secretary Hale, do you have any thoughts about it? Yes, it is not an easy challenge that the Army then has taken on, in terms of just making sure it can recruit and retain those that can meet the tests, whatever they may be. And to ensure that you have the capabilities you need across the force, as well, not just at the individual that is feeling well able to contribute at the highest level, but that you are also finding all the talent you need for the specific jobs, and you kind of align them properly.

General HAM. Yes, ma'am. I think that is right. And, of course, the requirements are changing. But I think we found certainly young people with highly technical educational backgrounds that are attracted to work in growing fieldings such as cyber defense and the like. And so looking for opportunities to match those skills and attributes that young people bring with the needs of the Army I think will be a vital component, again, to maintaining the excellence that the Army has achieved over many years.

And I would add just one other point is, the people who serve, they want to know that they are serving in the world's best Army. That requires a continued emphasis on leader development. It also entails a commitment to modernizing the force, to make sure that the soldiers are properly equipped to encounter any potential adversary.

Ms. TSONGAS. Thank you for your testimony.

I yield back.

Mr. TURNER. Dr. Fleming.

Dr. FLEMING. Thank you, Mr. Chairman. And, General, thank you for your service in uniform and your continued service in retirement, which is not so much of retirement. You are actively working now, and we thank you for that.

I was here earlier when you testified. And if I understand correctly, you said that 980,000 is really an absolute floor that we have to operate from. And I assume you also mean 450,000 for the Active Duty Component. Is that still correct?

General HAM. Doctor, that is correct. So that we were careful in the words that we chose. And so we chose that an Army of 980,000 broken down by components, 450,000 Regular Army, 335,000 National Guard, 195,000 in the Army Reserve, is minimally sufficient. We were careful about those words.

Dr. FLEMING. So it is really not even close to being ideal, where we really need to be on our manpower strength?

General HAM. We of course, we are not charged with recommending what might the ideal force be. It was, what was the force within acceptable risk and with anticipated resourcing? So that is how we came to that agreement amongst the Commission, that minimally sufficient was the right descriptor.

Dr. FLEMING. Would you comment on the fact that this administration's budget, because of increasing OCO [overseas contingency operations] needs, is now wanting to pull OCO out of base budget? Would you like to comment on that and what impact it has on this end strength number?

General HAM. Doctor, if you will allow me, I will make a brief comment and then look to the guy who understands this better than I do. I think one of the challenges with the overseas contingency operations funding is its lack of predictability, and that is why I think it is important to make sure that there is the right level and a predictable level of funding in the Army's base funding so that they can undertake many of the modernization efforts that are necessary.

As far as the impacts, let me turn to my partner here.

Mr. HALE. Well, the Commission focused on the minimum needed resources, and we really didn't look at how it ought to be funded. And I want to reiterate that we endorse the fiscal year 2016 plan, and we are not on that track now, as you know. The Army is significantly below those resources in this budget because of the Bipartisan Budget Agreement last year.

In terms of OCO, if I could follow General Ham and step away a bit from the Commission, it has the problems that he just said. You don't want to fund a lot of things in OCO because it is only one year at a time and the Department desperately needs to be able to look out over several years in planning programs.

That said, if the environment is such that it is the only way to go, at least I personally wouldn't turn it down. I think we have got to make things work.

Dr. FLEMING. Right, right, excellent. Also, again, back to you, General. The Commission cited the unstoppable OPTEMPO [operations tempo] within the Active Component a number of times throughout the report. Could the Commission provide some more specifics on what it found on the high rate of deployments, the current small size of the force, and how this has strained the Army?

General HAM. Yes, sir. Again, so we engage soldiers across the Army. We found the high operations tempo, rapid deployments below that level which is optimal for the Active Component, which would ideally be at least 2 years at home for 1 year operationally deployed, 4 or 5 years at home for the Reserve Components for every year mobilized or operationally deployed.

We found lots of units that were, particularly in the Regular Army, spinning faster than that, particularly in certain fields: aviation, missile defense, special forces, to be sure, and many others.

Part of that, the Commission felt, was due to the challenge in assured access and funding to allow Reserve Component units to perform many of those missions, which they are certainly perfectly capable of performing, but in some cases that requires a bit of additional funding to pay principally the salaries for those mobilized or activated Reserve or National Guard soldiers.

Dr. FLEMING. Right. Well, let me just say in ending here, I want to thank you again, General Ham, for your position on this, that this is an absolute more ragged edge, as we often say, that we cannot go below this floor. And, really, all things being said, really, we need to have better funding and more manpower.

But thank you.

And I yield back.

Mr. TURNER. Thank you. Mr. Walz.

Mr. WALZ. Well, thank you, Mr. Chairman. And thank you for putting the emphasis on this report that it deserves and pointing out some of the critical issues we are going to be tackling here. And to the Commission, I can't thank you enough for the work you did. On behalf of the co-authors, myself, Mr. Graves, Mr. Miller, Mr. Meadows, and former member Rahall, who put this in the NDAA, rarely have I seen since I have been here the letter and the intent, the congressional intent to carry it out the way you did it, and so thank you for that.

It was to inform us before we made decisions going forward. The number of people you went and spoke to, it is astounding. And I hear feedback all the time, and I want a special thank you from those National Guard folks out in Minnesota, that you took the time, you included them in this discussion.

And so when you are speaking of these issues, you are speaking exactly the way we are hearing it, about what they want to do, they want to be part of this team, they want—and we deserve to give them the best training, best equipment, and then integrate them into that fight. So thank you for that.

And it is on that that I would segue to, how do we do a better job? Did you come out of anything on that that maybe both of you—your opinions on this, General Ham—what do you think on integration?

We have tried this before. We tried integrating battalions in. We took troops out and leaders and embedded them at times. Certainly, over the last 10 years, the Guard has picked up their fair share of the missions and done them, but how do we go forward to ensure that this is a part of the strength we need?

General HAM. Congressman, I would offer two broad categories of how this might be enhanced in the future. One is, there has got to be from the very top leadership in the Army, from the Secretary of the Army and the Chief of Staff and the Sergeant Major of the Army, this continued emphasis on the total force. There is one Army. It happens to have three distinct interdependent, but essential components.

But as General Milley, the Chief of Staff of the Army, points out in many of his public addresses, over every soldier's breast pocket, it says U.S. Army. It doesn't say anything else. It says U.S. Army, irrespective of component. So I think that cultural emphasis by the Army's leadership is important.

Having said that, there are some matters in policy and even some in law that would help in the Commission's view to further the integration of the three components of the Army, such as the increased emphasis on the one Army school system, where, again, irrespective of component, your trained and educated the leader development programs for officers and noncommissioned officers are the same. You know, you grow up in the Army and you have different roles, so that is one area that we think a difference could be made.

And as I mentioned in my opening statement, some additional flexibility and, indeed, some additional resourcing in the section 12304b authority that allows for the employment of Reserve Component forces would be helpful, again, I think, in integrating the total force.

Mr. HALE. I couldn't agree more. The tone at the top is key. And I sense hearing General Milley speak, that he does want more integration, and we have heard that privately from him, and I have seen it in his statements. In addition to what General Ham said, there are a couple others I mentioned earlier. I think the Apache transfer itself is another way to help toward integration, as are multicomponent units.

I will mention two others that are in the report, one an integrated recruiting system. Right now, all three components have their own recruiting system, sometimes even competing with each other. The Commission recommended at least a pilot to look at integrating those.

And the Army right now does not have a single pay and personnel system that allows everybody to see each other's when the appropriate security guidelines, obviously. Integrated Pay and Personnel System–Army, IPPS–A, as it is called, is important I think to the overall integration. It is on its way. And I would urge that Congress fund it consistent with it meeting appropriate milestones, but treat it as a high-priority project.

Mr. WALZ. Well, I appreciate your thoughtfulness. And I said, it is to inform members of this committee and probably more importantly the folks who aren't on this committee that are in Congress. And I can't stress enough to my colleagues—I think many of us are concerned about these end strength numbers and we are concerned, as we rightfully should be, simultaneously on costs.

The Guard and Reserve is a way you can get your cake and eat it, too. And if it is done correctly, it has to be a part of this discussion.

And so I encourage us to continue to take these recommendations to heart and the work that you did will inform us as we go forward. You have done a great service, and I appreciate it.

I yield back.

Mr. TURNER. Mr. Walz, I believe you have a unanimous consent request for the committee.

Mr. WALZ. Thank you, Mr. Chairman. I appreciate that. I did have—the Reserve Officers Association, I ask for unanimous consent to put their statement in the record. They, too, pretty much echo that and thank you for what you did and talk about the one Army total force, so if I could submit that.

Mr. TURNER. Are there any objections?

Mr. WALZ. Thank you, Mr. Chairman.

Mr. TURNER. Without objection, the statement of the Reserve Officers Association will be included in the record. And turning to Mr. Gibson.

[The information referred to can be found in the Appendix on page 47.]

Mr. GIBSON. Well, thanks, Mr. Chairman. And I thank the ranking member, as well. Thank you for your leadership on this very important issue and holding this hearing. I also want to welcome in and stress my gratitude to both of our panelists today for their distinguished career serving our service men and women and their families.

You know, I want to echo the comments, certainly the work of the Commission. With regard to integrating the force, the total Army, I can recall back—although sometimes it seems like 1,000 years ago, being 17 years old and enlisting as a private E–1 in the Army National Guard, serving 5 years there, and then going in the Regular Army for 24 years, and then now on this side.

And while I think that there has always been good faith efforts to have this one force, I think that the weight of the Commission and Congressman Walz, highest ranking enlisted man to ever serve in these chambers, you know, and his team sponsoring this Commission I think is helpful, particularly when I see the Army leadership coming together and really wanting to do exactly this.

I think it is going to be really important, which leads to my next point, and that, Secretary Hale, I thank you for the work that you have done over your career on really bringing efficiencies, the reforms that are necessary, because as you both point out, I mean, we don't—end strength means very little if we have a hollowed-out force. We can't have that. We need to have fully trained, equipped, and ready force, and it needs to be rightsized, too, but all of that has to come together.

So towards that end, you know, I just want to build on some of the earlier testimony, and here I am just going to ask in your best professional judgment, General Ham, in your case, your best military judgment, when a BCT [brigade combat team] is stood down, and it is completed, how long does it take to turn the light back on?

Based on our experiences over the past decade, from the idea to the enunciation to the recruiting to the initial training to the integration in the unit, the training to the deployment into an operational area, how long is that period?

General HAM. Having some experience, Congressman, in doing this, having stood up an infantry brigade combat team while I was a division commander, I would say at the bare minimum, fully resourced, priority for manning, for equipment, and access to all the right training, I would say 18 months would be an absolute minimum, probably closer to somewhere in the neighborhood of 24 to 36, from a cold start.

Mr. GIBSON. Right. So that would be the unit. And I concur. I think that is most of our—and then of course you have—just to plan it in, you have to recruit. And then you have to actually get them to basic training and AIT [advanced individual training] and actually assess them into the unit, so it can take as long as 3 years, when you actually put that whole package together.

And that is what I wanted to really put into the record here, is that we are making decisions this year on end strength and for the American people to know that this is one that we assume a lot of risk. If we get this wrong, you know, it is not like, oh, well, you know, next month, we can just fix that.

If we draw down too far, you are looking at a 3-year lag time before we can even recur or we can regain that capability in our Armed Forces. And you acknowledge and agree?

General HAM. Congressman, I do. It is one of the reasons why we make a number of recommendations with regard to enhancing the readiness of the Reserve Components, but we also address the issue of expansibility, which has not gotten a lot of attention over the past several years, but there must be processes in place and plans in place so that in the eventuality where the Army is required to expand quickly, we know how to do that. And I think that requires some additional attention.

Mr. GIBSON. Indeed. And I noticed that in the Commission—and I think that was helpful. I will lay out a question now, but I then want to move—and we will see if we have any time we can recur back to it. But what I was interested from Secretary Hale is, you know, the analysis of given a scenario where we draw down and then we have to bring a BCT back on Active Duty, what does that cost in relation to whatever we think it is that we are saving?

But let me move on and see if we have time to go back to that. I do want to ask this question, and that is this. General, in your earlier statement, you talked about impact on troops and families. Thank you for that. And you know, you know, no one arguably knows that as much as you do. My point I want to get clarification for the record is that is assuming deterrence here. That is assuming, you know, we don't have to go fight one of these major theater wars.

If we had to go fight a major theater war, what would the impact then be on families in terms of dwell time? And what would that— because you know very well what that looked like in 2007, 2008, is troops ended up spending 16 months in theater and, you know, 11, 12 months back home, and then were rotating back.

So if you could for the record say what the impact would be on troops and families, if we do get committed to one theater.

General HAM. Yes, Congressman, I would commend to you and to all the members there is a classified annex to the report that addresses some of those issues in greater detail. But what I would say is that certainly in the case of a full-scale mobilization or commitment to a large-scale operation in any future theater or war, at the size of the Army that is anticipated, there is no dwell time. You know, for the most part, soldiers deploy and they are engaged for the duration.

This is a commitment on the parts of soldiers and their families to the defense of the Nation, and we have got to make sure that our support for them is commensurate with their commitment.

Mr. GIBSON. And I thank you. I think that is a very important point to enter into the record in terms of what the risk we are taking on for troops and families.

I will yield back. Thank you.

Mr. TURNER. Dr. Wenstrup.

Dr. WENSTRUP. Thank you, Mr. Chairman. I thank both of you gentlemen for your hard work and the information you have been able to provide us and give us some insight to all these very important matters.

I like to think a lot of times about our military force as being a deterrent for our adversaries in many ways. And I was wondering if you could weigh in and maybe comment on where our current state of the Army and military in general is serving as a deterrent to our adversaries.

And I know we have different types of adversaries today, potential adversaries. There is the peer to peer nation type adversaries and then there is the terrorist type adversaries.

But I wonder if you could comment on where you think we are today as far as being an effective deterrent to actions.

General HAM. Doctor, thanks for that question. I guess I would characterize deterrence in a couple of different ways. One is, in the purely military capability and capacity that the Nation possesses. That is measurable. It is accessible by force posture and levels of readiness. And that certainly shaped many of our recommendations, particularly with regard to posture overseas in Korea and in Europe, where there are a couple of different recommendations with regard to ground forces and Army aviation forces.

But deterrence also is based on elements of will and demonstrated capacity. It is one of the reasons why we think the presence of forces in Korea and in the case of Europe, we believe, the forward stationing of an armored brigade combat team conveys in very visible terms the will of the Nation to commit to deterrence.

Mr. HALE. Thank you. Let me just add a thought, and that is I think where the Army is able to deploy it is highly capable. This is a strong Army. The problem is more its capacity and can it do it in all the potential areas where they might be needed. I think that is the trade. The risks that we take is not having enough to do all of these requirements, meet all of these requirements. Where they are deployed, they are a capable force.

Dr. WENSTRUP. So what I am reading from that, General, especially your comments, when you talk about Europe, is we could be a greater deterrent than we currently are.

General HAM. Doctor, we make a recommendation that—it gets to the issue of, as this force, as this Army was sized and planned for the future, the strategic environment is different than it is today.

We did not—and most of the plans did not—we anticipated a very different relationship with Russia than what has evolved over the past couple of years. And we believe that that necessitates a relook, a rethinking of our overall strategy for employment of military forces for both deterrence, but also of assurance of our allies and partners.

Dr. WENSTRUP. I thank you both very much. I appreciate you being here today and the work that you have done.

I yield back.

Mr. TURNER. Gentleman yields back. We will go to Mr. Veasey.

Mr. VEASEY. Yes, I wanted to ask a specific question about the Commission considering the integration of women in the all-male ground combat units and what they think of the recommendations and, if so, what considerations are being made and determined on that issue.

General HAM. Congressman, let me start—let me ask Secretary Hale to comment. This obviously was not a specific charge to the

Commission. And the policy decision to open all specialties to women was made pretty late in the Commission's endeavors.

Having said that, we did have the opportunity to engage with leaders, with soldiers, both women and men, across the force and in all three components. And so we had some discussion about this. And I think the first response is one that won't surprise you, Congressman. It was from leaders at all levels that says, if the policy changes, because it was uncertain at that time, if the policy changes, we will embrace it and move out and apply the new policy to the best efforts that we have.

I would tell you, again anecdotally, in engaging with women, particularly young women, both enlisted and officers, there were mixed feelings about their personal interest in serving in the ground combat arms or other specialties which had previously been closed to women, but there was near unanimity in opening the opportunity to women who had the desire to serve in those specialties and the capability to serve in those previously closed specialties. I think we heard loud and clear that there was broad acceptance of the opportunity to do so.

Mr. HALE. I agree with what General Ham said. I mean, it wasn't a Commission issue, but speaking personally, I think it was the right decision. We need to harness all the capability we—or at least offer the opportunity to harness all the capability we can in the United States military, and this was a move in that direction.

Mr. VEASEY. Thank you, Mr. Chairman.

I yield back.

Mr. GIBSON [presiding]. Gentleman yields back. We will go to Ms. McSally, please.

Ms. MCSALLY. Thank you, Mr. Chairman. And thank you, gentlemen, for your service and your hard work on this Commission.

And I want to go back to the Apache transfer, and to be full disclosure here, the Silverbell Army Heliport is just outside my district, and many of the guardsmen live in my district. So any community is going to be concerned if they are hearing that, you know, something is going to change, we are going to lose those citizen soldiers from our community.

But aside from that, I am concerned about the operational impact of the executing this and then also the cost, as you mentioned. I have trained a lot as an A–10 pilot with the Apaches, tremendous location there with the weather and the airspace and the Barry Goldwater ranges, but it is a unit by itself.

So I am assuming if your recommendations are put into place, then we would lose that unit and that, you know, it would be located at some Active Duty Army base. So they would miss out on the operational strengths of being located where they are, so that is of concern to me, just because of the proximity and the airspace, the weather, the joint training opportunities.

But then also, as we have seen units sometimes go from Active to Guard or Reserve, you will see the expertise that we have of the pilots potentially flowing into the Guard and Reserve from Active Duty, so you can retain that expertise, but if you are going in the other direction, I am assuming you thought through—it is not likely to have a bunch of Guard pilots want to transition back to Active Duty. They have other jobs. They are rooted in the community.

So just the execution of that sounds very cumbersome to me. And also we might lose operational capability, certainly lose tremendous expertise if we go forward with your recommendations. It is not clear to me whether you are recommending with the four units staying in the Guard, would the training capability stay in the Guard and the operational capability be in Active Duty, just to clarify that?

And then I do want to clarify, obviously, there is cost that comes with that, so what was the logic behind making a recommendation that is increasing costs? And could you clarify again what those costs are?

General HAM. So I think let me start and then we will turn to Secretary Hale, who chaired the aviation subcommittee. Firstly, ma'am, we did not make any recommendations with regard to which units might be affected. We think that is left best to the Army.

We did, as the law required us to do, we did, in fact, actually look at the process by which Army National Guard forces are allocated amongst the States and territories and found with some minor recommendations, mostly administrative, that that process was pretty sound.

So I think the Commission has full confidence that if this recommendation is adopted, there is a good process to determine which units might be affected.

Secondly, let me say that the recommendation doesn't change the number of battalions that were intended to remain in the Regular Army. From the Aviation Restructuring Initiative, there will be 20 battalions, our recommendation keeps that same number in the Regular Army, but adds 4 battalions into the Army National Guard. That is over and above the Aviation Restructuring Initiative.

The intent was that those 4 Army National Guard battalions would be fully manned, but they would be equipped only with 18 by 24 aircraft. That is largely an acknowledgement of the added cost that would be required.

But when those battalions would be mobilized and operationally employed, they would cross-level amongst units, a practice which the National Guard is quite familiar with. Chief of the National Guard Bureau, director of the Army National Guard have advised the committee during its work that they are comfortable with that level of cross-leveling, so that when one of the four Army National Guard battalions would be operationally employed, it would go as a full-up battalion with its own personnel, but with aircraft from additional battalion—or from additional units.

With regard to the costs, let me turn to the cost expert.

Mr. HALE. We looked at four criteria before I get to the costs. One of them was cost. One, wartime capacity in a key scenario that is stressful to the Apaches. Second, a surge capability across a variety of scenarios. Third, how do they help in peacetime? Or how do they do in peacetime? And finally, costs.

I won't go through all of the options, but the Commission option ranked better of those that we looked in terms of wartime capacity, it had somewhat more surge capability than the Army's initiative.

And it offers some opportunity if these units are used, and we certainly hope they would be, to help in the peacetime, as well.

That brings us to cost. It does cost more, about $165 million a year in operating costs, and a one-time cost in procurement to manufacture more Apaches to the E model of about $400 million. We did offer offsets. They are illustrative. We recognize that and mentioned earlier they involve two fewer units of Black Hawks helicopters, the assault helicopter, and a modest slowdown in the modernization program for Black Hawks.

Black Hawks are important. But we felt that it was more important to have a balanced force with some more Apache capability, even if we had to pay for it through modest changes in the Black Hawk program.

So we tried to look at a broad criteria that included cost, but it wasn't solely cost.

Ms. McSALLY. So did the criteria include the potential loss of expertise and having to rebuild some of that expertise in the Active Army for the experience you will lose?

Mr. HALE. Well, as General Ham said, we would keep all 20 battalions that are currently in the Army, Apache battalions that are currently in the Army, so we shouldn't lose any capability there. It will be the same battalions and they will be recruiting for them. We would keep some ability for the Guard to be a repository of talent when Apache pilots leave, if they want to stay in the Guard, they would have the opportunity to do that under the Commission's proposal. So we would have some more capability there, but the same in the Active.

Ms. McSALLY. Okay, great, thanks. My time is expired.

Thank you.

Mr. TURNER. Gentlelady yields back. Ms. Bordallo.

Ms. BORDALLO. Thank you. Thank you very much, Mr. Chairman.

General Ham and Mr. Hale, I thank you both for your work on this informative Commission report. General Ham, a number of the Commission's recommendations focused on total force integration, preparing and leveraging the Reserve Component as an operational force, including increasing the annual number of Army National Guard combat training center rotations.

Now, if that were to be implemented, how can Congress ensure that the readiness built through the rotations is best maintained and best capitalized during the unit's on year, if these units are not deploying as they have in past years?

General HAM. It is a great question, ma'am. And you will allow me, let me offer an example that we came across. We visited the 116th brigade combat team based in Idaho, but with units from many, many different States, during their training at the National Training Center at Fort Irwin, California.

That unit, all of those units in that brigade had spent a considerable number of days, many more than the 39 minimum number of days each year. Some of those soldiers had 50 or 60 days in the year leading up to their National Training Center rotation. And they voiced the same concern that you did.

As they exited the National Training Center, at the peak of their readiness, they said, but we are going home. We want to be used.

We are trained. We are ready. And so that was a large part of why we recommended increased use of the 12304b authority, why we increased continued reliance on the operational capabilities that are resident in the Reserve Components of the Army, to capitalize on that investment in readiness that the Army had made.

The soldiers saw it. The leaders of that unit saw it. And I have confidence that the leadership of the Army, the Secretary and the Chief of Staff and the Sergeant Major of the Army are recognizing that, as well, and say we simply cannot afford to train units for training sake. We have to train and build readiness so that those forces can be operationally employed across the Army's needs.

Ms. BORDALLO. Thank you. Did you want to add to that?

Mr. HALE. I agree with that.

Ms. BORDALLO. All right. Thank you very much.

And I yield back, Mr. Chairman.

Mr. GIBSON. Gentlelady yields back. Mr. Bridenstine for 5 minutes.

Mr. BRIDENSTINE. Thank you, Mr. Chairman.

And thank you, gentlemen, for the great work you have done on the National Commission on the Future of the Army. I know we are going to hear from a lot of stakeholders on it, but I think on balance it is a lot of very good recommendations that this committee is going to have to take very seriously and move forward where we can.

I wanted to talk to you for a second about some of the short-range air defense and field artillery concerns. General Ham, the Commission found unacceptable shortfalls in the short-range air defense and field artillery. Fort Sill is in my home State of Oklahoma, the Fires Center of Excellence, and of course, it is the Army's home of air defense and artillery.

When you think about how important this is to the Army, a couple of things that were mentioned in the National Commission on the Future of the Army were the threats from unmanned aerial systems and cruise missiles. Could you maybe take some time and explain to this committee why it is so important that we make sure that we are taking into account short-range air defense and field artillery?

General HAM. Thanks, Congressman. First of all, I would commend to you the classified annex that has some further detail about the threats that are posed by potential adversaries in this domain. And I think it is important to this discussion.

At an unclassified level, I would go back to a previous comment that said when the Army that we have today was planned and structured, we did not envision the nature of the threat environment in which the Army must operate today. As one example, we did not anticipate that there would be many places in the world where the Army might operate where they would be subjected to threats by enemy air forces either manned or unmanned or cruise missiles. That is in large testament to the extraordinary capability of the world's finest Air Force to do that, but the threat situation has evolved.

And I would highlight particularly as we have seen integrated air defenses in Syria, as we have seen Russia's employment of both manned and unmanned systems in eastern Ukraine, it presents a different operating environment than that which was envisioned, and we believe that the Army needs to take note of that and restore some capability within the force to counter those measures.

Mr. BRIDENSTINE. So could you maybe share—is the concern on the shortfall, is it primarily modernization? Is it munitions? Is it manning? Is it doctrine? What is the—can you be more clear on what that shortfall might be? All of the above?

General HAM. It is a little bit of all of the above. It is structure and modernization. As one example, for very sound reasons, the Army has made a decision that all of its short-range air defense battalions reside in the Reserve Components. There are none in the Regular Army. At that time, that made a lot of sense. In our view, it doesn't make a lot of sense today, so there is a structure issue there, as well.

There certainly is a modernization component to this, as unmanned systems, smaller systems, more sophisticated adversary capabilities present themselves on potential battlefields, so there is a modernization aspect to this, as well.

Mr. BRIDENSTINE. One of the things we have heard General Milley say—he stated on multiple occasions that the Guard should get at least two additional combat training center rotations in this year's budget.

Do you agree with that?

General HAM. Congressman, we did not specify a number. We think that is best left for the Army. But we certainly do believe that it is—that the number of the Reserve Component combat training center rotations should be increased, importantly, but without diminishing, decreasing the number of Regular Army rotations.

Mr. BRIDENSTINE. Okay. Well, that makes—and you think it is possible to do more for the Guard and not decrease the Regular Army rotations?

General HAM. In our assessment, yes, it is.

Mr. BRIDENSTINE. Okay. One other question I had was the—the recommendation to eliminate two Regular Army IBCTs [infantry brigade combat teams], and ultimately did you consider other areas where you could find 8,500 people or how did you come to the assessment that infantry brigade combat teams is where that number needed to come from?

General HAM. Some of the details would be in the classified annex, Congressman, but in general, what I would say is that while infantry brigade combat teams certainly are stressed in any potential operational theater of war, they were less stressed than many other capabilities. And so we felt that we had to make at least some offer to say, if you have to make these very, very difficult decisions to increase some of the shortfalls in other capabilities, that this was a consideration, recognizing how difficult that decision might be.

Mr. HALE. We did look at a number of other potential efficiencies. We didn't study them in detail, but I think they—and they will be familiar to you. Most of them have been proposed. Health care reform, for example, the always difficult but important issue of closing unneeded facilities, and the integrated recruiting system that the Commission recommended—wasn't recommended primarily to save money, but it would potentially save some dollars. So we did look at some other areas.

Mr. BRIDENSTINE. Did you guys look at the Army service component commands, the nine different Army service component commands as a place to find personnel?

General HAM. We did look at the Army service component commands and spoke with them and with the combatant commanders that they support, but not so much in terms of potential space savings, while certainly there might be some utility in that, but it is important that the Army service components at least under current law and policy that is the mechanism by which combatant commanders access Army capabilities.

Mr. BRIDENSTINE. Right.

General HAM. So diminishing that brings some risk with it, as well.

Mr. BRIDENSTINE. And just real quick, did you guys look at Army Materiel Command?

General HAM. We did not take a deep dive into Army Materiel Command, principally because it is a largely civilian entity, so we didn't look at that as a potential space savings.

Mr. BRIDENSTINE. The chairman is telling me I am out of time, so I will stop.

Thank you.

Mr. GIBSON. Good work. Time's expired. We will go to Mr. Wittman, for 5 minutes.

Mr. WITTMAN. Thank you, Mr. Chairman. Gentlemen, thanks so much for joining us. Thanks for your efforts there with the Commission.

I wanted to begin speaking from my perspective as Readiness Subcommittee chairman in saying that I wholeheartedly agree with your recommendation number 7 in the report that says the Army must continue to treat readiness as its most important funding priority. That is in line with what we have heard from senior Army officials, including General Milley, the Army Chief of Staff, who has repeatedly said that readiness is number one and there is no other number one.

Secondly, I want to concur with recommendation number 14 that said the Army should forward station an armored brigade combat team in Europe. There is probably no other statement in the Commission's report that acknowledges the changed strategic situation in Europe better than that recommendation. And in your report, you quote EUCOM [European Command] commander General Breedlove as saying the virtual presence by U.S. forces will be translated by both friends and adversaries as actual absence.

And while we know the rotating U.S. forces into and out of Europe as we do now has significant value, we definitely need armor back in Europe, and that is needed because it is a credible deterrent to Vladimir Putin's ambitions.

The fact is, we have no armored units stationed in Europe anymore, and as I visited the Baltic states last summer to observe firsthand the impact of the European Reassurance Initiative, the prime minister of Estonia I think put it best when he told our delegation, deterrence is preferable to having to be liberated.

And with Prime Minister Roivas there giving us that perspective and having the longest period of time of independence for Estonia, I think those are very prophetic words.

And finally, like all of my colleagues, I have serious reservations that the size of the total Army, especially the Active Duty Army, is enough at the current levels being proposed to fulfill all of its missions. And the report states that for some potential challenges, the Army might have capability and capacity shortfalls and will be forced to deploy units not fully ready, which would not be acceptable, pretty plain and straightforward. On the next page, it states, even assuming full access to all Army components, this force size provides only limited ability to react to unforeseen circumstances.

And the report goes on to say that under current strategic guidance, the Army and other defense components are directed not to size themselves for large-scale, long-duration stability operations.

Yet the other direction is to conduct current stability and counterinsurgency operations, and that stated as one of the top elements in the joint force prioritized missions as described in the national military strategy of 2015. So those two statements are at counter purposes.

So not only is the 980,000 total Army at the minimum sufficient strength necessary to meet challenges of a future strategic environment, as stated in the report, it only barely meets that requirement when we wish away valid and required missions. And I think we have to be realistic about saying we can't change the mission sets to meet what we wish is provided for us on the resource side. And I understand wanting to try to take the 450 number and shoebox it into something that will fit, but I just don't believe that that is where we need to be directing this discussion.

My question is this. Is it safe to assume that if the Army had included sizing for stability operations the requirement for more IBCTs and enablers, that the number would be significantly higher than the 980,000 total recommended in the report?

General Ham.

General HAM. Congressman, thanks. So, again, the two parts of guidance in the law that were so important to us were size and force mix at acceptable levels of risk and consistent with anticipated levels of resourcing. So as I mentioned, if you alter one or both of those parameters, you would get a very, very different answer.

So if you were not budget constrained, I suspect the Commission would have come in with a much larger number. Or if you had said, you know, minimum levels of risk, you might get, again, a very, very different number.

I think, Congressman, what you speak to highlights the requirement to continually assess the evolving security environment in which Army forces will be applied. Again, in our judgment, the numbers are what we think are consistent with the charge that you gave us in the law. If you tinker with either of those, I think we would have had a very different outcome.

Mr. WITTMAN. Mr. Hale.

Mr. HALE. I would just like to repeat what I have said earlier. We are off track from even the Commission's recommendation in the latest budget. We recommended the fiscal 2016 budget request.

We are somewhat below that, probably $5, $6 billion below it for Army, and below it also for some of the other services.

So I think the first thing we need to do is try to get back on that track, and then we will go from there.

Mr. WITTMAN. Mr. Chairman, with your indulgence, I just want to ask one quick question with a yes or no answer.

Would you state then that under the current conditions we find today that an Army of 450,000 would be insufficient to properly manage risk and to address the threats we see before us today?

General HAM. If greater resources were available, I would agree with that. At the current level of resources, I will stand by the Commission's recommendation.

Mr. WITTMAN. Mr. Hale.

Mr. HALE. I agree.

Mr. WITTMAN. All right. Thank you, Mr. Chairman.

Mr. GIBSON. Gentleman's time is expired. We will go to Mr. Coffman for 5 minutes.

Mr. COFFMAN. Thank you, Mr. Chairman. I think my question to you is concerning pushing more capability to the Guard and Reserve to achieve cost savings. I think if you look at the costs of— I have read analysis where the cost of a sergeant E–5 in the Army, and if you take sergeant E–5 in the Reserve or Guard, that non-deployed it is about a third of the cost.

And then when you take—and that is discounting the legacy cost of retirement. And so that individual when retired will not draw until late 60 in the Guard and Reserve. And the Active Duty will draw—they could draw as young as probably 37, 38 years old, with 20 years in would be the youngest, probably certainly not the average.

And so I am just wondering, do we need a separate analysis? Or do you think you press that issue in terms of shifting capability to the Guard and Reserve in order to retain—to where we are obviously not compromising capability, but to kind of bend the cost curve in terms of personnel costs? I will start with General Ham, you first.

General HAM. Thanks, Congressman. We purposely did not seek to replow the ground that the compensation commission and others have looked at in this regard, but we certainly heard lots of testimony related to the points that you raised, that before mobilization or activation, certainly Reserve Component soldiers are less costly.

We looked at it from the Commission's standpoint more in terms of the operational capability that would be required to meet the Nation's objectives of the Army, and that is what led us to the force sizing recommendations that we made.

But it is important that 450,000 in the Regular Army, 335,000 in the National Guard, 195,000 in the Reserve is only sufficient if you properly train, modernize, and operationally employ those forces. If you put them on the shelf and don't modernize them, then the Reserve Components will not be ready to answer the call.

So it is—again, it is more than just the size number. It is the full package of training and modernization.

Mr. COFFMAN. I think you would—and I would agree with you, and I think you would have to restructure the Guard and Reserve in order to accomplish that. We don't want to go back to what happened during the first Gulf War where you had an entire I think Army national brigade that was deemed unfit to deploy. But I just think we have got to press that issue.

And maybe we have to rethink it in a broader way to where, do we want to maintain them as an operational reserve where they are going to be deployed to Active Duty maybe on an every 5 year basis or something like that for a limited period of time, as opposed to bringing them back to a strategic reserve and having a concern about their combat effectiveness being degraded?

Mr. Hale.

Mr. HALE. So you cited a common figure about a third. It varies to more like a third to two-thirds the cost. The aviation units are probably—in the Guard, even when not deployed, about two-thirds of the costs, or 60 percent, 70 percent as much.

But the key here is the Regular Army can do some things the Guard just can't realistically do. They can deploy early in a war.

I will use the Apaches as a good example, because we looked at them with care. We have got shortfalls in a key scenario early in the war, and only the Active—the Regular Army can help there. That convinced us to leave the number of Active battalions at 20.

But we are also short actually a little more later in the war. That is a capability that Guard can supply, and that is why part of the reason we recommended keeping four battalions of Apaches in the Guard.

So it is a capability cost tradeoff, as you know, and I think the Commission did its best and came up with the proposal that General Ham has discussed and I certainly share that that as being the right way to go.

Mr. COFFMAN. Again, you didn't take into—I agree with you that certain units are more expensive than others based on the Active Duty Component that is required to support the Reserve unit. But, again, we are not taking into account legacy costs, and I think that full analysis needs to be done in terms of cost.

And I also think that there are a lot of specialty areas that have a direct correlation to an occupation in the civilian world that don't necessarily—where we don't necessarily need that full capability except in a full mobilization. And yet we maintain surplus capacity on the Active Duty side. I am thinking about medicine as an example.

Whenever I go to Bethesda—when I went to Bethesda in 2011, there was a very significant patient flow there coming out of Afghanistan. When I go there now, they are looking for patients. And so we are treating patients from the Boston bombing. They were bringing in veterans with non-service-connected issues, just to try and maintain the certain level of capability.

And so I think that is something where we ought to look at plusing-up the Guard and Reserve and then bringing on when we mobilize.

With that, Mr. Chairman, I yield back.

Mr. GIBSON. Gentleman's time is expired. Ms. Tsongas for 5 minutes.

Ms. TSONGAS. Thank you, Mr. Chairman. I wanted to follow up on an earlier question and focus it a little differently. You know, as we are talking about end strength and what the proper number is, I think what we are all concerned with is the resiliency of the force and the pressures that come to bear, given the multiple challenges.

And I have seen in Massachusetts where there has been a lot of research investment in sort of making just better understanding as I said how you improve the physical, the psychological, the cognitive, the overall human performance of the force, with the interest of and understanding the inordinate number of pressures that come to bear on those who do serve.

And my question really is, do you see value in that going forward, as we are still—no matter what, but in a constrained environment, where we ask ever more of those who are serving, do you see value in that kind of research and development effort?

General HAM. Yes, ma'am. Absolutely. In two ways. One is simply from a readiness standpoint, we want to make sure that soldiers are as ready as they can be, and as you indicate, that is more than just technical or tactical training or other means of readiness, but it is readiness of the whole person that is vitally important. So I think from a purely readiness standpoint, that is quite important.

In perhaps a less objective measure, it is also I think integral to recruiting and retaining the quality people that we need, to know that when they raise their right hand and enlisted in the Army or are commissioned as an officer in the Army, that they are joining a profession that will attend to their needs and make sure that they are properly cared for and they are as capable and as ready to perform at maximum levels as is possible.

And it also sends a very clear message to their families that we will care for your soldier when the worst possible things that can happen to soldiers happen, that their families have confidence that the Army will take care of them in those dire circumstances. So for those reasons, I think the points you mentioned are absolutely essential.

Ms. TSONGAS. Thank you. Secretary Hale, do you—the other question is, we have been debating end strength here. And I think we are all concerned about what the appropriate number is. But if you look at the current situation, we have soldiers of the U.S. Army deployed in over 140 countries around the world. Some are obviously fighting, engaged in the fight. Some are there in a deterrence mode. Others are there just to reassure allies and partners.

And as we struggle with fiscal constraints, did you at all consider whether or not the Army is spread too thin? And is there better—should we be better channeling those that we do have in order to, for example, reduce the pressure on the deployed soldier and give them more dwell time? Was that part of your consideration?

General HAM. It was, ma'am. And in fact, the law required us to look at that. I think in a general sense, the Commission's view was one of the very best ways to alleviate the frequent operational deployments, particularly within the Regular Army, is to ensure that the Reserve Components of the Army are adequately trained, modernized, and prepared so that they can become more operationally employed.

It has the value of relieving a little bit of operational stress on the regular force, but it also builds operational capability within the Reserve Components.

And, ma'am, we heard loud and clear from those soldiers in the Army Reserve and Army National Guard that they have a burning desire to be operationally employed.

Ms. TSONGAS. So you didn't see it as sort of retooling what the Army should be doing and where, but rather how you do it and who you have do it?

General HAM. Well, it is certainly a mix of both. I think the demands from the combatant commands for the most part are increasing. There are systems within the Army and within the Joint Staff and the Office of the Secretary of Defense to prioritize and balance those demands. The demands will probably almost always exceed the supply, so it is a matter of prioritization.

And I think in general, the Commission's view was that if the Army can more effectively employ the operational forces in the Army National Guard and Army Reserve, that will go a long way toward meeting that demand and relieving some of the stress that is evident in some communities in the Regular Army.

Ms. TSONGAS. So you really didn't——

Mr. HALE. And I would just like to add to that, if I might, I fully agree. We need to use the Guard and the Reserve. We tried in the Commission to put our money where our mouth was on this one. For example, when we suggested keeping four battalions or recommended keeping four battalions in the Guard, we included in the costs the added cost to call them up on the one to five basis that is one of the planning scenarios.

And similarly, you have heard us say before we recommended more funding for this 12304b, which provides funds to call up the Guard and the Reserve.

We repeatedly heard that the reason they are not used more is not that they don't want to go. It is that there isn't the funds to pay for them when they are called to Active Duty. So we tried to, as I say, put our money where our mouth is. We need to use the Guard and Reserve, and we need to fund it.

Ms. TSONGAS. Thank you. I yield back.

Mr. GIBSON. Thank you. This concludes our questions. Any concluding remarks from our panelists? I will give you the opportunity at this point.

General HAM. Thanks, Mr. Chairman. I would conclude simply by again thanking you and Ms. Tsongas for the opportunity to come appear before the committee. And I would harken back to a comment Mr. Hale mentioned earlier in his testimony. The United States Army is the finest Army in the world. It has got some challenges, and we certainly need to be careful as we proceed.

But there should be no question that this is the premier land force on the face of this planet today, and that is thanks to the great women and men who every day choose to serve this Nation in uniform.

Mr. HALE. I would just like to take this opportunity to thank the guy to my right here. General Ham did a great job. He earned a merit badge in herding cats, which is one of the requirements if you I think are chairman of the Commission. He really did a good job in bringing us together and focusing on the key issues. So thank you. And thanks also to the staffs, some of whom are behind me, who did an outstanding job helping us get through a tough set of issues.

Mr. GIBSON. Well, I thank you both. And please do convey to all those on the Commission how much all of us here deeply appreciate their commitment to our country and the recommendations that they have provided.

And with that, that closes the hearing. Thank you very much.

[Whereupon, at 4:00 p.m., the subcommittee was adjourned.]

APPENDIX

FEBRUARY 10, 2016

PREPARED STATEMENTS SUBMITTED FOR THE RECORD

February 10, 2016

Statement of the Honorable Michael Turner
Chairman, Subcommittee on Tactical Air and Land Forces
National Commission on the Future of the Army
February 10, 2016

The hearing will come to order.

The subcommittee meets today along with Members of the Full Committee to receive testimony on the findings and recommendations of the National Commission on the Future of the Army.

I'd like to welcome our distinguished panel:

General Carter Ham, U.S Army retired, Chairman of the Commission, appointed by Chairman Thornberry, and

The Honorable Robert F. Hale, the Commissioner appointed by Ranking Member Smith. Mr. Hale was also the lead for the Commission's subcommittee on Army Aviation issues.

The Congress was prompted to form the Commission, in large part, over two major concerns.

The first was how the Army should best organize and employ the Total Force in a time of declining resources.

The second was whether the Army should proceed with the transfer of AH-64 Apache aircraft from the reserve components to the Regular Army as directed by the Army's Aviation Restructure Initiative (ARI).

The Commission reported its findings to Congress and the Administration on January 28, 2016, and made 63 recommendations, 19 of which were directed towards Congress for potential action.

This will provide the committee enough time to review the recommendations as the committee prepares to markup the National Defense Authorization Act for Fiscal Year 2017.

In considering recommendations, the Commission was instructed to take into account "anticipated mission requirements for the Army at acceptable levels of national risk and in a manner consistent with available resources and anticipated future resources."

Consequently, the Commission assumed that the Army budget is flat lined at the FY16 PB levels (with inflation).

The Commission has indicated that a "Total Force" Army of 980,000 soldiers is an "acceptable level of risk," but is the lowest total end strength the

Army can go given mission requirements and the current Defense Strategic Planning Guidance. Again, the commission did not consider the potential for budget increases over the FY16 PB.

However, the Commission did acknowledge that the current Defense guidance does not include emerging threats such as Russian aggression and the growth of ISIL.

The Commission then further notes that perhaps "their greatest concern is the inadequacy of that guidance"…

We've heard senior military leaders testify before this committee that our military is operating at the "ragged edge" and that current assumptions in the defense guidance are "rosy" at best.

Here's what we know.

- The Army is being asked to do more with less.
- Demands from the Combatant Commands for Army capabilities and capacity continue to increase;
- The world security environment is considerably worse now than when the Department conducted its most recent quadrennial defense review in 2014. Going beyond just Russia and ISIL, North Korea conducted another ballistic missile test over the weekend.
- The Army has soldiers deployed in over 140 countries.
- The Army has provided over 1.5 million troop-years to the wars in Iraq and Afghanistan since 2001
- The Army has nearly 100,000 soldiers committed to the Pacific. and continues to deter aggression in the Korean peninsula.

However, despite these demands the Army has continued to downsize and budgets have been reduced.

I commend the commission for developing and recommending risk reduction strategies to help the Army mitigate risk given the current budget constrained environment, but Congress has the responsibility to make the hard choices.

It's obvious to me that the Administration and DOD need to revise and update current defense guidance that clearly addresses the threats we now face.

For example, General Breedlove recently issued new theater strategy for the U.S. European Command that now has its number one priority as deterring Russian aggression in Europe.

I hope today we can engage in candid discussion regarding total Army force capability and capacity as compared to current and emerging threats.

I want to briefly touch on the Army's aviation restructure initiative or ARI.

Originally the ARI had proposed numerous changes to Army Aviation Capacity, including the transfer of all Apache helicopters out of the Army National Guard to the Regular Army.

The commission examined three comprehensive options for the Army's ARI and we look forward to hearing more details about their final recommendation.

This should also provide a great opportunity for the Committee to gain a better understanding of the Commission's views in how to better utilize the Reserve Components.

Before we begin, I would like to turn to my good friend and colleague from Massachusetts, Ms. Niki Tsongas, for any comments she may want to make.

Statement of Gen. (R) Carter Ham
Chairman, National Commission on the Future of the Army
Testimony before the House Armed Services Committee
Subcommittee on Tactical Air and Land Forces
February 10, 2016

Chairman Turner, Representative Tsongas; on behalf of all my fellow commissioners, thank you for inviting me and Commissioner Bob Hale to testify before the committee on our report on the future of the Army. We appreciate the opportunity discuss our findings and recommendations with the committee.

The Committee and staff have already received the Commission's report, so I won't spend a lot of time addressing specific points. But, I would like to give you a sense of how comprehensive we were.

The Commission made every effort to be inclusive, accessible, and transparent.

We visited 17 states and interacted with:
- over 320 different Army units;
- all 54 Adjutants General and 33 Governors
- about 80 Members of Congress; and
- all six geographic Combatant Commands and many of our most important allies and foreign partners

And that is just a very partial list.

I should also point out that we paid strict attention to the law you passed creating the Commission; you'll notice every chapter begins with a direct quote from the law as a way to frame the subsequent material.

The result is a set of 63 specific recommendations that are unbiased, well researched, based on realistic assumptions, and backed by solid data. Importantly, our recommendations had to be consistent with "acceptable levels of national risk" and "anticipated future resources." In other words, we were not unbounded in our work.

What we found is that our Army is the best in the world. Those who wear the uniform deserve our gratitude every day.

But the Army faces severe challenges, most of them budget-driven. From fiscal years 2010-2015, overall defense funding declined 7%. Army funding declined 14%.

On the two main issues before the Commission – force size and mix, and the Apache transfer – the Commission found the following.

An Army of 980,000 is the minimally sufficient force to meet current and anticipated missions at an acceptable level of national risk. Within that 980,000, the Commission finds a Regular Army of 450,000, an Army National Guard of 335,000, and an Army Reserve of 195,000 represent the right mix of forces and, again, the *absolute minimum* levels to meet America's national security objectives.

To fully understand this recommendation it is important to remember the mandate you gave us. We weren't asked to come up with an optimal force size based on the world situation and our best judgment. That would have been nice, but it would not have been realistic.

Instead, we were asked to size the force in light of the two previously mentioned considerations – acceptable risk and anticipated resources. Adjust either or both and you can arrive at very different conclusions, and I'm sure you and the administration will have your own ideas on how to balance those considerations.

However, in our assessment, an Army of 980,000 is the absolute minimum – a floor, not a ceiling.

On the Apache question, the Commission recommends the Army maintain 24 manned Apache battalions – 20 in the Regular Army and

four in the Army National Guard. The Commission recommendation has advantages over the Aviation Restructure Initiative in both wartime capacity and surge capacity, and will reduce peacetime deployment stress. It will also promote better integration of the Regular Army and National Guard.

To offset the added cost of having four Apache battalions in the Guard, the Commission suggests the Army could add only two Black Hawk battalions to the Guard instead of the four currently planned, and slow Black Hawk modernization.

The report also contains several prominent themes based on the Commission's fact-finding and analysis.

First, the All-Volunteer Force is a national treasure. Since its inception, the quality and professionalism of the force has improved dramatically – but it is expensive. However, the Commission considers sustaining the All-Volunteer Force vital to the future of the nation. All budget and force management decisions must be made with this goal in mind.

Second, the Commission believes it is critically important to develop a true "one Army" Total Force culture. While the Regular Army, Army National Guard, and Army Reserve are distinct, essential, and interdependent, they are meant to operate as one force – with their efforts fully integrated.

The Commission found that gaps and seams exist in the implementation of the Total Force Policy. The report highlights some of those and offers remedies.

For example, we recommend putting all Army marketing under one roof, fielding a consolidated pay and personnel system, and making changes to the existing 12304b authority that will make it easier for the Army to employ the reserve components.

And third, the Commission recommends funding at the president's FY16 level, which would provide the Army with the *minimum* resources necessary to meet its requirements at acceptable risk. But given the strategic environment and potential for growing instability, even this funding level may prove inadequate.

Furthermore, it should be understood that even with budgets at the PB16 level, the Army would still suffer from significant shortfalls, in aviation and short-range air defense as well as other capabilities we address in the report.

That is a very brief rundown on what we found. Certainly, not everyone will agree with our recommendations. Indeed, many have already voiced their disagreement.

What I do hope, though, is that our report will contribute to the important debate that the Congress and the Administration, indeed the Nation, must have to determine how America's Army should be sized, trained, modernized and postured.

With that, we are prepared to answer your questions.

# # #

GENERAL CARTER F. HAM, U.S. ARMY RETIRED
CHAIRMAN

Appointed by the Chairman of
the House Armed Services Committee

General Carter F. Ham served as the Commander, U.S. Africa Command from March 2011 until his retirement in June 2013. His previous assignment was Commanding General, U.S. Army Europe.

General Ham began his service as an enlisted infantryman in the 82nd Airborne Division before attending John Carroll University in Cleveland, Ohio. He was commissioned in the infantry as a Distinguished Military Graduate in 1976. He is a graduate of the Naval College of Command and Staff and the Air War College.

In addition to numerous stateside assignments, he served in Italy, Germany, Kuwait, Macedonia, Saudi Arabia, Qatar, and Iraq. His duties with USAFRICOM took him to 42 of Africa's 54 nations. His General Officer assignments included Commander, Multinational Brigade Northwest, Mosul, Iraq; Deputy Director for Regional Operations, J-33, The Joint Staff; Commander, 1st Infantry Division; and Director for Operations, J-3, The Joint Staff.

Since retiring from the Army, General Ham has worked as a consultant with SBD Advisors in Washington D.C. He serves on the Board of Directors for John Carroll University, the Board of Directors of Aegis Defense Services LLC, the Board of Global Nexus Alliance, and on the Africa Board of Advisors for Jefferson Waterman International.

THE HONORABLE THOMAS R. LAMONT
VICE CHAIRMAN

Appointed by the President of the United States

Thomas R. Lamont served as the Assistant Secretary of the Army for Manpower and Reserve Affairs from June 2009 to September 2013. In that capacity, he was the Army's point person for policy and performance oversight of human resources, training, readiness, mobilization, military health affairs, force structure, manpower management, and equal employment opportunity. He is currently a principal at LAMONT Consulting Services in Washington, D.C.

Prior to his appointment as Assistant Secretary of the Army, Mr. Lamont was the chairman of the University of Illinois Board of Trustees and a longtime Springfield, Illinois, attorney concentrating in government law and legislative affairs. He is admitted to practice before the U.S. Supreme Court, the U.S. Court of Appeals for the Armed Forces, U.S. district courts, and Illinois state courts. He served as a judge advocate general in the Illinois Army National Guard, culminating his 25-year military career as the Illinois Staff Judge Advocate and retiring as a colonel in 2007.

Mr. Lamont received his bachelor's degree from Illinois State University in 1969 and earned his law degree from the University of Illinois College of Law in 1972.

SERGEANT MAJOR OF THE ARMY RAYMOND F. CHANDLER III, U.S. ARMY RETIRED

Appointed by the Ranking Member of the Senate Armed Services Committee.

Sergeant Major of the Army Raymond F. Chandler III was the 14th Sergeant Major of the Army from March 2011 until his retirement in January 2015, serving as the Army Chief of Staff's personal adviser on all enlisted-related matters, particularly in areas affecting soldier training and quality of life. He traveled throughout the Army observing training and talking to soldiers and their families. He sits on several councils and boards that make decisions affecting enlisted soldiers and their families.

Sergeant Major of the Army Chandler entered the Army in Brockton, Massachusetts, in 1981 and graduated as a 19E armor crewman from One Station Unit Training at Fort Knox. He has served in all tank crewman positions and has had multiple tours as a troop, squadron, and regimental master gunner. He was the Command Sergeant Major in 1/7 Cavalry, 1st Cavalry Division (OIF II 2004–2005), U.S. Army Garrison Fort Leavenworth, the U.S. Army Armor School, and the U.S. Army Sergeants Major Academy (USASMA). In 2009, he became the first enlisted Commandant in USASMA history.

He has a bachelor of science in public administration from Upper Iowa University.

GENERAL LARRY R. ELLIS, U.S. ARMY RETIRED

Appointed by the President of the United States.

General Larry R. Ellis served as Commander, U.S. Army Forces Command, from November 2001 until his retirement in 2004. His prior assignment was Deputy Chief of Staff, G-3 Headquarters, Department of the Army. Since 2013 General Ellis has been President and CEO of VetConnexx, a company that provides career opportunities for veterans.

General Ellis earned his commission through ROTC at Morgan State University and held a number of command positions over more than 35 years, starting with company commander in the 82d Airborne Division at Fort Bragg and the 101st Airborne Division in Vietnam. He served as Commander of Multinational Division (North) in Bosnia and Herzegovina, and 1st Armored Division in Germany. His staff assignments included Deputy Director for Strategic Planning and Policy, U.S. Pacific Command, and Deputy Director, Military Personnel Management, Office of the Deputy Chief of Staff for Personnel. He also served on the faculty at the U. S. Military Academy, West Point.

General Ellis earned a bachelor of science in public health from Morgan State University and a master of science in public health from Indiana University.

THE HONORABLE ROBERT F. HALE

Appointed by the Ranking Member of the House Armed Services Committee.

Robert F. Hale was the Under Secretary of Defense (Comptroller) from 2009 to 2014, serving as the principal advisor to the Secretary of Defense on all budgetary and fiscal matters. As the Department of Defense chief financial officer, Mr. Hale also oversaw the department's financial policy and financial management systems. Prior to serving as defense comptroller, Mr. Hale was Executive Director of the American Society of Military Comptrollers. Mr. Hale currently is a Fellow at Booz Allen Hamilton, serving as an advisor to corporate leadership.

Early in his career Mr. Hale spent about three years as an active duty officer in the U.S. Navy and another five years in the Naval Reserve. He also spent several years as a staff analyst and study director at the Center for Naval Analyses. He then joined the Congressional Budget Office, where he headed the National Security Division for 12 years. From 1994 to 2001, Mr. Hale served as the Assistant Secretary of the Air Force (Financial Management and Comptroller).

Mr. Hale graduated with honors from Stanford University with a bachelor of science in statistics. He also holds a master's degree in operations research from Stanford and a master of business administration from George Washington University.

THE HONORABLE KATHLEEN H. HICKS

Appointed by the President of the United States.

Dr. Kathleen Hicks served as Principal Deputy Under Secretary of Defense for Policy from 2012 to 2013, responsible for advising the Secretary of Defense on global and regional defense policy and strategy. Prior to that she served as Deputy Under Secretary of Defense for Strategy, Plans, and Forces, leading the development of the 2012 Defense Strategic Guidance and the 2010 Quadrennial Defense Review. From 1993 to 2006 she was a career civil servant in the Office of the Secretary of Defense, rising from presidential management intern to the Senior Executive Service.

She currently is senior vice president, Henry A. Kissinger Chair, and director of the International Security Program at the Center for Strategic and International Studies (CSIS), where she previously worked as a senior fellow from 2006 through early 2009. She also is an adjunct with the RAND Corporation and a member of the Council on Foreign Relations.

Dr. Hicks received her doctorate in political science from the Massachusetts Institute of Technology, a master's from the University of Maryland's School of Public Affairs, and a bachelor of arts magna cum laude and Phi Beta Kappa from Mount Holyoke College.

LIEUTENANT GENERAL JACK C. STULTZ, U.S. ARMY RETIRED

Appointed by the President of the United States.

Lieutenant General Jack C. Stultz served as Chief, Army Reserve, and Commanding General, United States Army Reserve Command, from May 2006 until his retirement in 2012. Upon assuming command of the Army Reserve, he retired from Procter and Gamble as an operations manager with 28 years of service. He currently serves on the Board of Directors of VSE Corporation in Alexandria, Virginia.

He received his commission through ROTC at Davidson College in 1974 and eventually served as Commander, Company B, 20th Engineer Battalion. He transitioned to the Army Reserve in 1979 and served with the 108th Division (Infantry OSUT), the 32d Transportation Group (Composite), and 143d Transportation Command, becoming commander in 2004.

He deployed to the Gulf for Operation Desert Shield/Desert Storm in 1990, to the Balkans for Operation Joint Endeavor/Joint Guard in 1997, and to Kuwait in October 2002 as Commander, 143rd TRANSCOM (Forward), moving into Iraq with the initial ground offensive and establishing a forward logistics hub at Tallil and rail operations at Garma. In 2003, he was assigned as director of movements, distribution, and transportation, Combined Forces Land Component Command Kuwait.

GENERAL JAMES D. THURMAN, U.S. ARMY RETIRED

Appointed by the Chairman of the Senate Armed Services Committee.

General James D. Thurman served as Commander of United Nations Command, Republic of Korea-U.S. Combined Forces Command, and U.S. Forces Korea from July 2011 until his retirement in October 2013. Prior to that he served as Commanding General, U.S. Army Forces Command, and was Deputy Chief of Staff, G-3/5/7. He is currently the president of JD Thurman Enterprises, LLC in Salado, Texas.

He earned his commission through ROTC at East Central Oklahoma University in 1975. His combat assignments include battalion executive officer in the 1st Cavalry Division during Desert Shield/Desert Storm; the Chief of the Plans and Policy Division for Allied Forces Southern Europe in Kosovo from 1999-2000; the Chief of Operations for the Coalition Forces Land Component Command during the invasion of Iraq; and the Multinational Division Commander responsible for all coalition operations in Baghdad in 2006. He also served as Commanding General of the National Training Center, the 4th Infantry Division at Fort Hood, Texas, and V Corps in Germany.

He holds a bachelor of arts in history from East Central Oklahoma University and a master of arts in management from Webster University.

DOCUMENTS SUBMITTED FOR THE RECORD

FEBRUARY 10, 2016

RESERVE OFFICERS
A S S O C I A T I O N

Reserve Officers Association of the United States

Statement for the

House Armed Services Committee

Subcommittee on Tactical Air and Land Forces

Hearing on the

Report of the National Commission on the Future of the Army

February 10, 2016

"Serving Citizen Warriors through Advocacy and Education since 1922."™

Reserve Officers Association
1 Constitution Avenue, N.E.
Washington, DC 20002-5618
(202) 646-7700

The Reserve Officers Association of the United States (ROA) is a professional association of commissioned, non-commissioned and warrant officers of our nation's seven uniformed services. ROA was founded in 1922 by General of the Armies John "Black Jack" Pershing during the drawdown years following the end of World War I. It was formed as a permanent institution dedicated to national defense, with a goal to inform America regarding the dangers of unpreparedness. Under ROA's 1950 congressional charter, our purpose is to promote the development and execution of policies that will provide adequate national defense. We do so by developing and offering expertise on the use and resourcing of America's Reserve Components.

The association's members include Reserve and Guard Soldiers, Sailors, Marines, Airmen, and Coast Guardsmen who frequently serve on active duty to meet critical needs of the uniformed services. ROA's membership also includes commissioned officers from the United States Public Health Service and the National Oceanic and Atmospheric Administration who often are first responders during national disasters and help prepare for homeland security.

President:
Col. James R. Sweeney II, USMC (Ret.)   202-646-7706

Executive Director:
Jeffrey E. Phillips   202-646-7726

Legislative Director:
Lt. Col. Susan Lukas, U.S. Air Force Reserve (Ret.)   202-646-7713

DISCLOSURE OF FEDERAL GRANTS OR CONTRACTS

The Reserve Officers Association is a member-supported organization. ROA has not received grants, contracts, or subcontracts from the federal government in the past three years. All other activities and services of the associations are accomplished free of any direct federal funding.

STATEMENT

ROA applauds the comprehensive report of the National Commission on the Future of the Army (NCFA). We will focus our comments on issues that directly affect the Army's Reserve Components – the Army Reserve and the Army National Guard. We begin by making three general observations and then move to several specific observations and recommendations.

GENERAL OBSERVATIONS

ROA strongly supports the overarching conclusion of the report that the Army must implement the Total Army Policy and develop a culture that embraces the concept of "one Army." We also endorse the implicit findings of the commission that the two Army reserve components have distinct but complementary missions – the USAR under Title 10 and the ARNG under Title 32 – and should be maintained as separate entities.

The All-Volunteer Force is key to the future of the Army. Maintaining this force for the future will require requisite resources. It is also critical that future force management decisions in personnel and finance ensure systems are fully integrated. They must create an environment in which soldiers can more easily move between assignments and components. The goal should be to create a true continuum of service process that will permit the Army to attract and retain high quality people through different stages of their careers.

With the high optempo of the force, especially the Regular Army, use of multi-component units should be fully reviewed, and creative alternatives explored through pilot programs. The ultimate goal should be full integration to the degree that the unique constraints, as well as capabilities, of Citizen-Soldiers are accommodated.

It is true that many RC Soldiers are trained, competent, and prepared to be mobilized on a regular basis. It is also true that many RC Soldiers have civilian jobs or other obligations that conflict with repeated mobilizations. Regardless of their patriotism or ardor for service, they cannot be both frequently deployed and succeed in their "day jobs." We must strike a balance among these differing realities within our force if we are truly to make best use of the precious human resources wearing the uniform of our nation.

SPECIFIC OBSERVATIONS

In offering observations, we caution that we are still digesting the work of the commission; we are also working with the Army leadership in a collaborative discussion with its Reserve

Components and other military service organizations serving the Army's readiness. In our experience, this collaborative approach between military officials and advocates is as rare as it is essential – it's what this town should do more of, and we applaud the Army for doing so . . .

Within that context and its constructive potential to further shape our thoughts, we offer some early observations on the "Developing One Army" recommendations. Generally we concur with the remaining recommendations.

> *Recommendation 29: The Congress should expand 12304b authority to include operational requirements that emerge within the programmed budget timeline, including the year of execution.*

To more fully use the RC for operational support, the present authority to use the RC under Title 10, Section 12304b, must be more flexible and be expanded. As currently written, 12304b permits mobilization of units as long as the mission is preplanned and funded. However, the timeframe for this use – planning two years in advance – precludes employment of the RC for emerging missions for which they are ideally suited. Missions suited for the RC could include theater engagement and security assistance.

> *Recommendation 30: The Army should budget for and the Congress should authorize and fund no fewer than 3,000 man years annually for 12304b utilization of the reserve components. The Secretary of Defense, in conjunction with the Army and the Office of Management and Budget, should also provide for the use of Overseas Contingency Operations and supplemental funding for reserve component utilization under 12304b.*

The proposal to authorize and fund 3,000 man years is a good start, but more is needed. The 3,000 man years would not sustain even one brigade combat team for a year. We suggest that immediate, further study by the COCOMs for the resources they might need and use is necessary. The demand by ground force commanders is regularly exceeding availability – modification of 12304b could go a long way toward resolving that issue.

> *Recommendation 35: Congress should enact legislation to allow assignment of Regular Army officers, NCOs, and enlisted soldiers to Army National Guard positions to execute all functions without prejudice to their federal standing. The legislation should also permit the similar assignment of National Guard officers, NCOs, and enlisted soldiers to Regular Army units.*

We support the concept that Regular Army officers, non-commissioned officers, and enlisted soldiers be assigned to full-time support positions in the USAR and ARNG. These assignments should be in addition to current AGR positions. It would do the units no good if current AGR slots were simply eliminated and replaced by Regular Army personnel. The USAR in particular is understaffed, with about 75% of authorized strength; it is urgent that this shortfall be reduced. Today's systems for equipment, personnel and finance, and audits are exceedingly complex and it is unreasonable to ask units to meet the various recording keeping and archival demands with part-time Troop Program Unit soldiers. Although reasonable checks and balances are well and good, the demands for many layers of approval for routine actions seem excessive, especially in a system that is undermanned and undertrained to perform these complex record keeping functions.

> **Recommendation 47**: The Army should reduce mandatory training prescribed in AR 350-1, Army Training and Leader Development by the following means:
> a) Reducing the number of mandatory training requirements and moving the reduced tasks to local command policy per AR 600-20, Army Command Policy;
> b) Developing a formal process for approving additional mandatory training tasks and reviewing existing mandatory training requirements annually for retention or deletion;
> c) Chartering the Army's Training General Officer Steering Committee to provide governance for approving all added Army and Combatant Commander mandatory training requirements;
> d) Changing the reserve components' mandatory training requirements from an annual cycle to a two-year cycle;
> e) Codifying mandatory training requirements with (1) task, condition, and standard; (2) Training and Evaluation Outline and lesson plan; and (3) the means to make this information available through the Army Training Network as the consolidated repository for mandatory training requirements;
> f) Delegating mandatory training exception approval authority to two-star commanders; and
> g) Completing the AR 350-1, Army Training and Leader Development, revision within one year of this report.

Recommendation 47(a) would change the Reserve Components' mandatory training requirements from an annual cycle to a two-year cycle. A two-year cycle is a welcome change that we think will enhance unit readiness and preparedness; among other benefits, it permits the force to focus more of their drill time on mission essential tasks.

> **Recommendation 48**: The Army should resource First Army's Active Guard and Reserve (AGR) positions from the Army National Guard and the Reserve at the aggregate manning level provided for each component not later than FY17.

We support the recommendation that the Army resource First Army RC positions at the aggregate manning level provided for each component. This is an excellent way to achieve multi-component success.

ROA RECOMMENDATIONS

We would like to bring to the House Armed Services Committee's attention some items that were, in the "crowded hour" of the commission's time and resources, not directly addressed:

- Integrate senior RC Army officers and NCOs into the Army Staff and open up more command positions for qualified Army Reserve officers, including three-star deputy AC command roles.
- Expand ways in which Guard and Reserve officers and NCOs can achieve Joint Qualified Officer status. For example, give them full credit for experience when assigned to the joint staff and create more options to fulfill their schooling requirements. US Army War College non-resident students should be able to augment their normal studies and achieve the Level II accreditation needed for JQO status, which they cannot now do. To ROA, the qualification apparatus of JQO operates as a "priesthood," excluding with needlessly difficult qualifications the meaningful participation of the Reserve Components. This exclusivity robs reservists of the opportunity to serve and it robs the nation of excellent joint warriors at a time of increasing need. In so doing, this elitism frustrates the intent of the Goldwater-Nichols Act.
- Increase possibilities for Regular Army officers to do tours with major Guard and Reserve commands, enhancing inter-component understanding and interoperability.
- Demand proof of full integration of USAR units into disaster response planning. This would ensure accountability and recognize the key role USAR units could provide in Defense Support of Civil Authorities (DSCA) operations. It is a mistake to think that in DSCA the two RC components would be in competition: their strengths are complementary. Undervaluing the considerable benefits that USAR units can supply communities in the event of a disaster means overlooking a valuable resource that can save lives and preserve communities.
- Create a new category of Reservist to embrace the "super subject matter expert" that may be needed by senior commanders. The notional name is not meant to connote an elite, but to identify the concept of extraordinary expertise not customarily resident in the force – which is not "grown" by the Army Military Operational Specialties and schooling system. Current laws and regulations provide some relief in this area but they should be reviewed and expanded to meet the needs of the Future Force.

CLOSING

ROA applauds the commission for its work in producing the final report and for its initiatives regarding the Army Reserves. Properly used, the Army's Reserve Components can contribute in training, education, and on the increasingly complex and diverse field of battle. The RC brings essential capabilities to the Active Component, especially within combat service support units that are under-represented or do not exist in the Regular Army. These capabilities require resources, such as adequate full time support personnel to properly administer these complex systems.

America's Reserves are not the nation's free defense lunch. Adequately resourced, as they have since the Guard's advent in the 17th century, Citizen-Soldiers provide our nation a unique and affordable augmentation of its military capability.

We appreciate the opportunity to submit this statement and to serve those who served us so well.

www.ingramcontent.com/pod-product-compliance
Lightning Source LLC
Chambersburg PA
CBHW081421280526
45788CB00009B/3190